# IT'S A NEW DAWN
## New Beginning

## WOMEN OF DISTINCTION
*Women Making a Difference*

PUBLISHING ▲▲ COMPANY

# REACH THE PRESS

Reach The Press Publishing
14051Belle Chasse Blvd Unit 213
Laurel, Maryland 20707


Printed in the United States of America

# Carolyn A. Ayers

# THANK YOU

*Jesus, for the new beginning and the dawning of a new day to leave my past* **BEHIND AND** *moving forward* **TO EXCITING** *and* **AMAZING** *new* **ADVENTURES.**

# OPEN DOOR

Today
I close the door
to the past, open
the door to the
future, take a
deep breath,
step on through
and start a new
chapter in my
life.

# IT'S A NEW DAWN

*This book is devoted to all of those who are at a turning point in their life. And looking to start a new Venture take the leap of faith. Through the power of the Almighty God who will help you reach your destiny*

# It's A New Dawn

SUDDENLY I
JUST KNOW IT'S TIME
TO START SOMETHING
NEW AND TRUST
THE POWER OF GOD
FOR NEW BEGINNINGS

*Open Door*

# INTRODUCTION

To Ms. C memoir a collection of memories as she writes about her childhood and life. Highlighting how Jesus Christ never left her on her journey. Ms. C centered her book on specific parts of her life. She covered a critical turning point in her life and particularly memorable stories of touchstone events. Ms. C is about to walk through that door call retirement, and she wants this adventure to be a fantastic venture. So, she is putting all her mistakes behind her. After reaching adulthood realizing that she had to forgive her father if she wanted God to forgive her for all her mistakes; was a turning point in Ms. C's life and she made an effort to forgive her father according to the Well of God with the help of the Holy Spirit.

# TABLE OF CONTENTS

# TABLE OF CONTENTS

# ACKNOWLEDGMENTS

To my Lord and Savior, Jesus Christ;

Thank you for an opportunity to reflect on my life in this literary treasure, and for giving me Prophet Michael Allen Ayers Sr., First Lady Charlene R. Ayers, Pastor Wilbert Ayers Jr., and Co-Pastor Debra Ayers.

I am forever thankful to be blessed with a loving and supportive family who continues to be my strength and inspiration: My mother Mrs. Josephine Gilbert Ayers, a Prayer Warrior and Intercessor; my sister Evangelist Wanda Denise Ayers;

# ACKNOWLEDGMENTS

my daughters, and their husbands, Prophetess Lakiesha, and Robert Thomas, Sr., Prophetess Quiana, and Minister Cedric Wingard, and La'Shone and Marques Anderson, Sr.; and my son and his wife, Allen II and Shenelle Tillman.

Finally, I want to acknowledge the nine beautiful grandkids that the Lord has blessed me with: Robert Jr., Ronnie, Royal, and Rhea Thomas, Marques Jr., Markel, and Mariah Anderson, Christian S. Tillman and Chloe L. Wingard.

and so
the
adventure
begins

# *FORWARD*

Opening the door and walking into retirement is going to be a change and a new beginning. Change is inevitable.... Growth is a process... Transformation comes to all of us-whether we prepare for it or not. Our lives are in a perpetual state of transition. Life always moving forward; nothing ever remains the same. To move forward, you have to leave yesterday behind. There is no standing still because time brings about a change. To some degree, we are continually changing--whether suddenly or gradually--into the new, the different, the unexpected, or the inexperienced.
Everything in this world changes from one era to the next age that is the decree of life. If you don't transform your life; your life will change you. The only persistent in life is change. The process never ends until you breathe your last breath. We need to remember that yesterday is our past, tomorrow is a secret, today is a gift of God, that's why we call it the present.

Matt. 6:34 says this: "Take therefore no consideration for tomorrow: for tomorrow shall take the view for the things of itself."

After all, our Heavenly Father knows what we need. Live today. Live in the now, Live in the present, by practicing God's presence every moment of every day. Rejoice in the Lord. This is the day that the Lord has made. Let us rejoice and be glad in it. As we move throughout this life, God is in the business of maturing us. As we grow, His demands on our life change.

God's plan is Flawless - Nothing we could add to God's blueprint would improve it. When He reveals His will to us, we need to recognize that God sees the end of the problem before the trouble begins. He knows the road we will take, and He knows the obstacles and valleys we will pass through as we go through life. His ground plan cannot be perfected, but it must be followed for there to be victory and blessing! I can't be in no better place than the perfect will of God for my live. So, the confidence of living a holy life comes down to God having control of my mind, my body and When God calls a person, it requires trust and obedience to follow him. It is not merely a call to a new way of life; it is a call to a new kind of life.

This level of uprooting and total change can generate concerns and be scary and stressful. Whatever your age, no one saved from growing. How do we grow from youth to adolescence to maturity? You will not instantly be mature.

Maturity is a lifelong process, As newborn babes, desire the sincere milk of the word, that ye may grow thereby; (1 Peter 2:2). Feed daily on the Word of God. That's where your strength lies. Saturate your heart and life with the Word. Maturity is living in Christ-likeness. (Colossians 1:28).

Perfect doesn't mean sinless; it means mature. You can be young only once, but you can be immature for a lifetime — many people who've been born again but cease to flourish. Jesus said "I am the vine; you are the branches. If you remain in me and I in you, you will bear much fruit; apart from me, you can do nothing. (John 15:5) Jesus spoke of Himself as a Vine, and we are His branches. He tells us that the branch is to abide in the vine, and then there will be growth. Jesus also shows us how to change and improve our selves to become what God wants. In John 15:7 Jesus said: "If you remain in me and my words remain in you, ask whatever you wish, and it will be done for you." Jesus said the same thing in John, "you will know the truth, and the truth will set you free" (John 8:32).

 The only way to replace the error of the world's way of thinking is to replace it with God's truth, and the only infallible source of God's truth found in his revealed Word, the Bible. God's Word must fill our minds. Jesus prayed, "Sanctify them in the truth; your

Word is the truth" (John 17:17). Moses said to Joshua "This Book of the Law shall not depart from your mouth, but you shall meditate on it day and night, so that you may be careful to do according to all that's written in it. "For then you will make your way prosperous, and then you will have great success." (Joshua 1:8).

As I walk a new path, I'm closing the door to my past and to my working career. I'm looking forward to the road that God has mapped out for my future. Believing that my journey will be prosperous and I will have great success.

# TODAY
# I HAVE
# THE POWER
# TO CHANGE MY LIFE

today,
I have
the POWER
to change my
story.

As a Child
I always wanted to grow up
Not realizing that A

# BROKEN HEART

Can find you there too.

# Childhood Memories

As I approach retirement looking back at my life, I see a new dawn. I was born in New Orleans, Louisiana in Charity Hospital to Josephine Gilbert Ayers and Wilbert Ayers Sr.  My mother was a tranquil person and loving, and my father was a quiet person as well when he was sober. He was a violent man once he became drunk. I remember as a child being terrified when my dad walks through the door on the weekend.  The weekdays he would go to work come home and watch the news and western movies. During the week the house would be calm but the after effect of the weekend the house did not feel like home just quiet.

My father felt that giving me an allowance every two weeks could make up for the terror he had put me through that weekend. My dad made sure I had money from the age of 8 years old until I was a young adult and able to work; he gave me an allowance. The money was a way for me to get out of the house and go to Canal Street to shop, but it did not make me happy.  As a child, I did not know what happiness was. I felt like a child that was just existing. As a very young child, I was frightened and terrified to move. Many times, I just wanted to hide under the bed or in the closet.

When I became an adolescent, I was angry and very vocal to my dad and anyone else that approached me in an ugly way. As a young adult, I would talk back to my dad sometimes. I'm not proud of it because I would not want my kids to talk back to me. One time in the kitchen I remember talking back to my dad regarding how my dad was so violent to my mother and he slapped me in the face.

When I reached adulthood, I was really lost when it came to being a loving and affectionate person when it came to a relationship with a man. That was because I hated my dad I thought he was a horrible person. What kind of man would fight a woman? That made me not have confidence in the men in my life. Childhood should be a happy and pleasant time in a kid's life. Childhood in a typical household is an unforgettable time full of stories that are both fun and touching. I don't have memories of special enjoying times like those. I do remember going to school at five years old and playing on the playground. When we were done playing, we would go into the classroom, and my teacher would say it's naptime in kindergarten. We all had to lay down and take a nap. I remember having a few childhood birthday parties.

I also remember at nine years old sitting on the front porch with my god-sister Janice Combre and my siblings, and we are thinking that something was going on inside the house where we lived because the lights seem to go off and on. Remember we were kids and for me being afraid as a small child had become the norm for me anyway. The only pleasant things I can remember as a child was watching television my favorite cartoons were Flintstones and Popeye and watching movies the three stooges and bonanza. These programs will tell my age because only people my age will recall these shows.

My mom tried her best to make us comfortable she kept our home immaculate you could eat off the floor the house was so clean. She would have breakfast and a hot cooked meal for us every day during the weekdays.  On the weekend she would make us breakfast, lunch, and dinner. During the holidays she would get us gifts, and she made sure that we had the best clothes and shoes. That is one thing my mom made sure that we had a place to stay, food and clothing.  My dad made sure we had food he would go to the French Market and get fresh veggies and fruits.

In our house, there were no Friday night movies. With popcorn and a beautiful blanket where the whole family would get together and watch a video. How I wish that would have been the case, but it wasn't. Friday through Sunday our home was like a war zone. My father would be fighting my mom, and I had to watch and feel helpless.

My thoughts of childhood are a child needs to feel loved by both parents. They should be surrounded by care and affection. A child should feel safe, and their learning process should start at home. There is no replacement for love; it is the most important thing. If that isn't shown right from the very beginning, then everything that follows is playing catch up trying to make up for all that is missing. My mom was very loving and affectionate, and she cared about us having shelter, food, and clothing.  My father cared about us having food and being around family.
He made sure that we knew our cousins, aunts, and uncles. Looking back my parents loved me in their own way, but I would have instead had a home with peace, joy, laughter and the sense of feeling safe. Babies come into the world anew, without all the baggage, sadness or anxiety that the parents carry. Babies, unfortunately, cannot pick their parents.

I think childhood is a time to learn with the help of their parents. Youth is about learning how to make friends and in school working together in a group. It's about imaginative play, sharing stories. Things like that will ground you in the human experience of loving kindness that you will pass on. The communal experience is also essential for a child, and that could be reading a book with their parent, watching television together as a family. This will help you as a child to be able to come together with different generations at diverse functions.

I was brought up in a dysfunctional household where there was no encouragement for asking questions. The ability to think of home as a place where ideas can be cultivated is critical, but that did not happen in my house. As a young adult, you have a voice, but I was not able to express my view. My parents did not have the skills on how to hear my voice and offer the space and opportunity for it to grow. My mom was a Christian, and she taught me about the virtues of diversity and about racist behavior and for me not to fall prey to that type of behavior. She taught me that there are people of different languages and people with different experiences.

In closing this chapter on my childhood; ultimately, the family is a collection of stories, and youth is an introduction to that book. As you live your life, you come to realize the significance of that introduction is everything, and it affects all aspect of your life.

Life without Jesus
is like a broken pencil...

no point!

# WALKING TIME BOMB, AN ANGRY CHILD

As a teenager, I was a walking time bomb an angry child. No one knew not my parents or my siblings; it was a quiet storm going on inside of me. As a teenager, I was busy trying to make sense of the physical changes happening to me, as well as the changes in my emotions and sometimes moodiness. Just like other emotions, frustration is perfectly natural and it is neither right nor wrong to feel angry. But how our passion manifests itself can be hurtful, scary and detrimental. Just like pain, anger itself can have an important function to tell you that what is happening is not acceptable and that something needs to change.

Feeling irritated is a warning sign that essential needs aren't being met, a push towards making changes or a way of showing other people how we think and what we need to happen but sometimes you're too afraid to make that push. It can be challenging to deal with the intense emotions that you feel when you're angry. Feeling angry and not expressing it can make you feel powerless and helpless, it can make you ill and have aches and pain.

That is what happen to me as a teenager because of me keeping anger locked inside of me when I had my monthly cycle I would have awful pain unbearable pain where I would fall on the floor because the pain was so intolerable. I know that teenagers can have childhood tantrum and show anger because of an argument they're having with a friend, and they just need a listening ear.  You as a parent ask them something, and the teenager seems to push you too far, and the argument and conflict seem a bit like a childhood tantrum.

When young people have intense feelings, often they are not able to think straight or listen to logic. They get flooded with emotions.  But for me, my anger came from my environment and not being able to express how I felt having to keep all my feelings bottled up inside.  That made me be like a walking time bomb.  I was not a bully or a person who go around and pick a fight, but if someone said one wrong thing or made one wrong move, it would set me off.  Parents should listen to their children and take responsibility for things they might want differently from them and not get angry and upset when they express how they feel. Like I said I did not have that opportunity to have those kinds of talks with my parents.

You see I let my father's anger become my anger as strong feeling can be infectious; it is crucial not to make that happen.  If I only had someone that would have tried to understand what was really going on beneath the surface, to help me work out what I was really feeling, and what it was that I needed. Just the act of listening to me would have helped to lower my emotional temperature in those moments of frustration.

Parents should realize that their action affects their children. They should try to understand their teenager's feelings and needs and why they act the way they do. A very long time I did not speak to my dad he would come home from work and say good evening, under my breath I would say what is good about it.  My mom would talk to me about it and tell me that it is no way for me to act with my dad, but she never asked me why. Just the act of her asking me why and listening to me would have help because what a parent thinks their child might be feeling could be entirely different. My mother thought it was about my allowance, but that was not the case because money at that time in my life was not important to me.  The turmoil that was in our home was the thing that was bothering me.

After the stormy times of me mouthing off to my dad when I calmed down, I wish that one of my parents would have acknowledged the painful and robust feelings I had been experiencing. To help me work out how I was feeling, what I needed, what they could do to help me express such feelings in the future and get what they need without me hurting them and myself. I felt from young that parents should allow their kids to express themselves and they should be recognizing and accept their feelings and needs.

Unfortunately, for me, that did not happen as I have expressed repeatedly. I had questions about feminine changes and the things that a young lady needed to know regarding these changes (female stuff). My mom told me the basic stuff about womanly things. The intimate details I learned later in life. But as a parent, I tried my best to recognize that my kids had feelings and gave them the opportunity to express themselves. Because I never forgot how I felt not being able to say mom leave my dad I would rather eat bread and water then to see you abuse like this. Words I never got an opportunity to speak....and the anger builds.

 In my late teens, I felt trapped between my childhood and ever-growing adult opportunities, working, driving and career choices. Even though I still needed my parent's guidance, I sometimes found it unpleasant. During one rebellious encounter with my father, I screamed, "I hate you"! Still, nothing was done or said to help me deal with this anger locked up inside of me. Even though most parents mean well and have the best intentions toward their kids, there are still times when they don't treat their children with respect they deserve as human beings, and they are unknowingly unfair. This was the case with my parents, and it causes me to be an angry teen.

Because of my anger, I fought in school. As I told you earlier, I was not a bully but if I was approached it lit a fuse. One day in Gym class at Carter G. Woodson High School when I was in seventh grade, a young lady approached me regarding her boyfriend. I told the young lady I'm not interested in boys and I do not have a boyfriend. So, if she had a problem regarding her boyfriend, she should confront him. Will she didn't like that answer and she hit me. That was too bad for her because she didn't know that I was a walking time bomb. My teacher and classmates had to pull me off the young lady.

There was other time at the same school in the same grade during another class a young man touch my leg. Maybe the young man liked me and was trying to be friendly but too bad for him he lit that fuse and again my teacher and classmates had to pull me off the young man. I was not afraid if it were a boy, girl, man or woman if they approached me wrong it would set me off. My Homeroom teacher at Woodson High called me out of my name because she said I was friendly with so many boys at the school and that was not good in her eyes. I did not use foul language, never did, my dad did that enough for me, but I was sassy, and I told the teacher off. I was suspended for three days from school, and that teacher did not want me back in her class. My dad gave me a whipping for being suspended not realizing that he was the cause of my actions.

Yes! I got along with boys better than girls when I was in high school, but they were just my friends. They would carry my books for me, and I did not discriminate whoever wanted to carry the books I allowed them to do so. I did not wish just to have one of my friend's carrying my books then he would get the wrong idea and think that he was my boyfriend. At that time in my life, I had so much hurt and pain locked inside of me that was the furthest from my mind having a boyfriend.

I recall another incident with a young boy at the park around the corner from our house we live on Washington Ave uptown. The young boy was bullying my brother Wilbert. When I found out, I when to the park and confronted the young boy.

I told him if he put his hands on my brother again he would have to answer to me. I said let me hear you touched him again it is not going to be nice, and you can take that to the bank. There was one more incident that happens I was around thirteen, and there was a white male at our front door when I open it. I asked the person whom you're looking for, and he said your father is your parent home. As I told you, I was not afraid of the person if it was an adult male/female or a child boy/girl. I did not answer the question. I just asked him are you looking for Mr. Ayers. The white male said yes, is Mr. Ayers home. Again, I did not explain to him I only with off on the man. I told him you have the nerve to come to my father door looking for money your company has more money than my dad will ever have and I need you to get away from this door and don't come back. That was disrespectful for a child to react in that matter but as I said I was a walking time bomb. I never told my dad that the man came to inquire about his bill.

That was to save me from the consequences. I would just like to say as parents we should not intentionally cause our kids to feel unwanted, controlled, manipulated or ignored. We should not make promises that we can't keep, be unrealistic in our expectations and avoid intimidation, bullying or comparing your kids.

Try listening and avoid using your children to meet your own needs. If you think you as a parent has contributed to your teen's frustration, remember no one is a perfect parent. With humility, hope and God's guidance, there is always the opportunity for change. Because God created the family, He desires that you grow in your love relationship with your teen. This may mean journeying through some unfamiliar and perhaps frightening new relational territory by learning to communicate freshly.  The main thing to remember is to keep the communication lines with your children or teenager open.

*Keep moving beyond my Past*

*Look forward to my future…*

It's A lack of

*Love and Forgiveness*

And

It's A lack of

*Friendship*

That makes

UNHAPPY MARRIAGE

# *MY ROCKY ROADS*

The rocky roads in my life were my three fail marriages.  I will not blame my dad, but I will say that he did not show me what a happy marriage involved. It is hard for me to talk about marriage because of being divorced not one time but three times. I thank God for his Grace because there is no condemnation of me being divorced. Because if I asked Jesus Christ to forgive me of my sins, He is faithful and places my sins in the sea of forgetfulness. Let's talk about how the Lord intended marriage to be.  Marriage according to the Word of God gives Christians hope that a husband and wife, by intentionally choosing to learn how to love faithfully and sacrificially as Jesus did, may keep their covenant promises for a lifetime. Marriage was instituted by God as the union of one man and one woman for a lifetime, and its value is timeless because it serves as a reflection of God's love and commitment to His people.

But in reality, Christian or not, marriage is difficult for any couple to sustain over a lifetime. Life's trials-the pressure of making a living, of parenting, of resisting temptations to unfaithfulness or selfishness-can strain any marriage.

My first marriage, one that I should have stayed in because first love is forever loved.  Reflecting on my childhood and what I saw in marriage there was no grey area for me, no comprising it had to be perfect are I was out of there. An ideal marriage is where I was so wrong because there is no perfect marriage. That was my biggest mistake thinking that a man or a woman could be perfect. I was young and foolish to believe that there were no grey areas in marriage. Will, my first husband, was the youngest in his family and he was familiar with that type of treatment. I was the oldest in my family, and I had to be responsible for handling business because my mother was in and out of the hospital due to all the physical abuse.

So, my husband didn't use to pay bills like I did so we had a financial issue (money problems). I was willing to overlook that and go to work and help but what hurt me so bad that I could not get over was at the time we lived in Atlanta Georgia, he was writing a young lady back at home in New Orleans, Louisiana that was his girlfriend back in high school.  That was bad but not the worst of it I found the letters under a stack of newspapers in our bedroom closet.  I maybe could have gotten over the letters because he was there with me in Georgia. The young lady was in Louisiana, but it was what my husband said in the letters as I sat and read them how my husband wishes that he was there with her, how he made a mistake getting married and how much he loved her. Here I had three little girls for him I was heartbroken. I did not seek God in the situation, and it took me down rocky roads.

I left Georgia and when back home to New Orleans and I had to find a job to take care of my three girls. I began to work at Charity Hospital where I was born, and this is where I meet my second husband. He was very nice to my girls, but he was controlling when it came to me. He would transfer the house phone where it would not ring so that I could not talk with my mother and siblings because at that time my father had passed. He would spend money and buy things without discussing it with me. He put me through mental abuse with his manipulation about my salvation and attending church. He cheated on me with the lady that he is now married too. But out of this marriage, God gave me a son whom I'm so very proud of and blessed to have. He and my three girls have been a blessing to me, and now I have one daughter-in-law and three son-in-law's that I'm so blessed to have.

I do have some happy memories of working at Charity Hospital. I meet some wonderful friends, and we started a birthday club, these amazing ladies where Charlene, Herlinda, Ella, and Louisa we had some exciting times together celebrating each other birthday.

We would get each other a cake and have some refreshments and enjoy spending time laughing and talking. Very memorable and enjoyable times for me.

My third marriage was the worst; this relationship was abusive from the start, and I should not have put myself or my kids through the abuse. The devil was trying to cause me to lose my mind and my life but God. I had given my life to Christ, and I wasn't that angry teenager at this time in my life because if I were still that person, I would have killed my husband, and God knew. I was mentally distressed and my husband he would be abusive to me in our bedroom or when the kids were not around. One morning I was stress and was not focus and almost was in a car accident and could have lost my life on my way to work. This man was verbally abusive and physically abusive. I check into a battler woman shelter in New Orleans, Louisiana my family and kids did not know that this was where I was I made up a story. Then I visit my friend in Tulsa Oklahoma, Louisa Bab because of the abuse and this man said that he would not ever be abusive again that was a lie. My friend told me she does not believe him he is lying to get you back in New Orleans and she was correct. Once I was out of the marriage, I saw a glimpse of that dawning shining through.

If you're reading this book, know that husbands and wives should love each other with genuine, sacrificial love. They accept each other's faults and shortcomings (not controlling nor abusive). They should be concerned with the other's growth and fulfillment. They should respect and honor each other. To be passionate about freedom and liberty for one another. Husband and wife should freely offer forgiveness-even before it is requested. They should love one's husband or wife the way Christ loves his church. In the covenant of marriage, the partner mutually gives of themselves for the other. Marriage is not a relationship in which one partner may dominate the other, or one partner enjoys great freedom while the other suffers in servitude. Marriage is a relationship of mutual love and sharing, so that mutual fulfillment may abound. Marriage is about keeping your marriage brimming with love in the loving cup. Whenever you're wrong, admit it. Whenever you're right shut up!

The three little words most often associated with marriage are "**I Love you**." Certainly, love is essential to the marriage covenant. But the covenant of marriage is built less on love than it does on three other little words. "**I forgive you**." Christian marriage thrives on gracious forgiveness.

It is through mutual and continuous forgiveness that husband and wife become heirs of the grace of life.

Ephesians 5:21-33 says, be subject to one another out of reverence for Christ. Wives, be subject to your husbands as you are to the Lord. For the husband is the head of the wife just as Christ is the head of the church, the body of which he is the Savior. Just as the church is subject to Christ, so also wives ought to be, in everything, to their husbands. Husbands, love your wives, just as Christ loved the church and gave himself up for her.

To make her holy by cleansing her with the washing of water by the word, to present the church to himself in splendor, without a spot or wrinkle or anything of that kind-yes, so that she may be holy and without blemish. In the same way, husbands should love their wives as they do their own bodies. He who loves his wife loves himself. For no one ever hates his own body, but he nourishes and tenderly cares for it, just as Christ does for the church because we are members of his body. For this reason, a man will leave his father and mother and be joined to his wife, and the two will become one flesh.

As I close this chapter on my rocky roads to avoid going down that rocky road in your life. If you're married and your husband or wife is not abusive, mentally or physically but he or she has faults forgive him, or her, be patient with him or her if he/she is not mature.

These are the things I did not do in my first marriage, and I paid dearly for not following the Word of God on marriage instead  I reflected on the things that happen in my childhood with my parents and it cause me even more pain and hurt.

EVERY
NEW DAY
IS ANOTHER
CHANCE
TO CHANGE
YOUR LIFE

# Believing in the Storm

When I was twelve years old, I found out that Jesus Christ would answer prayers. When my mother was given up by the doctors from Colon cancer at Tour Hospital in New Orleans, Louisiana. They told my dad to call the family together because my mother was not going to live. I prayed and asked God if He would let my mother live and not die. I told God, I heard in church that He answers prayers. If He was real and could listen to me and answer my prayer. Well God answered my prayer because my mother is still with me today and she is eighty-eight years old.

From sixteen until I got married, I was a great Christian girl, such a sold-out missionary for God, such an inspiring Jesus-follower. I'm not saying I did not make mistakes, but my heart was the focus on how God had moved for me and how powerful God the Father and Jesus Christ the Son was in my life. But then the bottom had fallen out of my life. Actually, it was much worse than that; the bottom had dropped out of my life, and I did not call on God like I did when I was twelve. Significant transitional changes mingled with months of physical exhaustion. Isolation and loneliness were heaped on top of a desperate struggle to find meaning again. I was left in an unbelievably depressive cycle I had lost my dad, and my marriage was falling apart.

I was a shell of the person I had been. After fighting on my own awhile, I'd thrown myself at the mercy of God. But this time, even He wasn't there. Heaven itself was silent. My sad, angry prayers echoed back into my ears, noisily. My tears slunk to the floor, uncaught, unwiped. I sobbed, mutely, into my pillow. If no One was listening, I didn't want to hear it either. I used to have daily Bible study times, then all I could stomach is to say the Our Father Prayer. I used to have it all put together, now all I was is angry over the tiniest things. Used to do so much good kingdom work, now all I do is menial tasks. I used to be so balanced and healthy, now I was one millimeter away from total depression.

Used to help so many other people, now all my energy is self-focused just to get myself through the day. After going through my second divorce and now in the third marriage. I was utterly broken; doubly broken because of the shame and guilt and fear of being violated. Christians aren't supposed to be dejected! They're supposed to be well and whole, godly servants of others and, well, happy in the joy of the Lord. Because I did not seek God as I should have in my marriages. It would be many months that turned into years before I would see glimmers again of light in the darkness that had become my life in my third marriage that was abusive. When it came, it came slowly, gradually, like a sunrise.

It first warmed my mind, my circumstances, and my perceptions – then methodically plodded its way into the depths of my very heart. Once I realize that God moved for me before and he would again if I would whole-heartedly believe. I began to have better days. I heard myself saying, "On my better days, I know that God is my deliverer."

Eventually, the light returned fully. The sadness was gone, but I was surprised to find that the humbleness remained: steadfastly, beautifully, whole-heartedly, and respectfully. My wound had been healed, and I was still broken. In this new light, I could see that the brokenness was the healing. I was free from this depress place I had put myself in by marrying this person who was abusive to me. I was safe to admit my faults, I was at liberty not to take my mistakes too seriously, and I could dive more in-depth in my relationships with Jesus Christ than I ever had. Why I was not going to focus on my mistake so severely was because I had asked God the Father and Jesus Christ the Son to forgive me of all my mistakes.

Jesus places them in the sea of forgetfulness. Accepting my brokenness was my humbleness before the Lord and His power. I turned myself and my sins into glorious tiny teardrops, and it turned His cross and His grace into the beautiful ocean in which I was now covered with grateful forgiveness.

Indeed, God was who I thought He was. He wanted me to bring Him everything, most of all everything in prayer. Spiritually, formative, and repentantly I had turned a blind eye; I had hidden it from myself. That I needed Jesus Christ in my life all along, but due to my charting my own course I turned a blind eye. So when it forced itself to the surface, it was like lava from an invisible volcano, buried deep, exploding through, breaking upward, re-making itself into my life as a new reality. I was also surprised to find in my heart – alongside and intermingled with the brokenness – profound freedom and a brimming reservoir of gratefulness that Jesus Christ had never left me.

Growing up in the church gave me the faith to believe in the power of an Almighty God. I was blessed and ordained by the Late C.L. Samuel, who was Pastor of Temple of Prayer Ministries and License by Prophet Michael Ayers Sr., General Overseer, Keep Your Eyes on the Lord, Outreach Ministries, Anderson, South Carolina. I attended fellowship with my brother Prophet Wilbert Ayers Jr. General Overseer, Temple of Prayer # 2. I also attended church at Pastor Arthur L. Thomas, Mount Carmel Baptist Church, Rev Matthew McGarry, Second Zion Baptist Church # 1 and Pastor Freddie H. Dunn, New Hope Baptist Church all in New Orleans, Louisiana.

At present, I'm a member of Dominion Church at Joy House, Pastor Edward Olds, General Overseer, Laurel, Maryland. For the past eighteen years, I have been living in the Metro DC area I have grown closer to Jesus Christ, and that jubilation of light is shining brightly in my life.

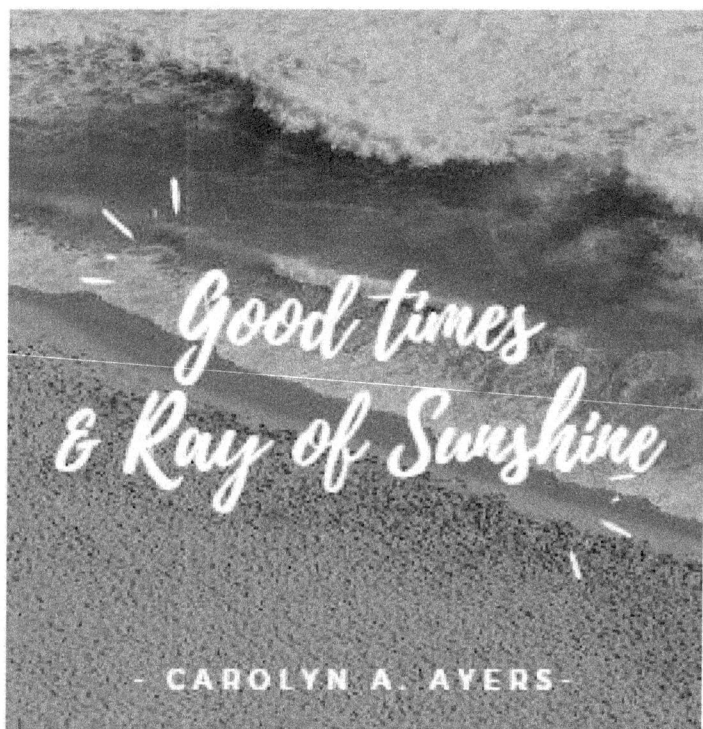

Good times
& Ray of Sunshine

- CAROLYN A. AYERS-

# *Ray of Sunshine*

Jesus Christ is my ray of sunshine, and He showed forth His brightness in my life when I received the news that I was selected for a position in the Metro Washington, DC area as a Paralegal for the Department of Veteran Affairs. That was a ray of sunshine a place and time in my life that brought me happiness after going through a difficult situation and my third divorce. I moved from New Orleans, Louisiana with my dear friend Margaret Ann Pierre, who told me, Carolyn, I'm going to relocate to DC would you be interested in tagging along. She was that someone that person who made my life happier as a dear friend.

 Along with my faith in Jesus Christ that He would be with me in this transition. I'm so grateful for the invite because it changed my life. As the year's pass, I am coming more and more to understand that it is the ordinary, everyday blessings of our typical daily lives for which we should be particularly appreciative. They are the things that fill our lives with comfort and our hearts with gladness. Just the pure air to breathe and the strength to breathe it; just warmth and shelter and a place that feels like home; just everyday food that gives us energy; the bright sunshine on a cold day; and a cool breeze when the day is warm."

When I move to the east coast my son was in college, and my girls were all married and had relocated away except for one, my oldest daughter at that time was still living in New Orleans, Louisiana. My second oldest daughter was in Germany with her husband, and my youngest daughter was in Delaware with her husband. So, I was all alone in the Washington, DC area. My siblings and my mom also were still in New Orleans. It was so beautiful to come home from work to a peaceful and pleasant home not just quiet but warm and cozy. It was quiet because I lived alone but this quiet time was much more different than in my childhood.

My lifeline was my walk with God; it was my faith in God. Learning to thank God for the bad times as well as the good times is an attribute produced by a strong belief in the knowledge that God does all things very well. For all the Lord had done for me, there was a tremendous need for me to purpose in my heart not to defile myself or compromise my beliefs with the world. Personal convictions will be tested. Many folks live for God until things get a little rough, then they want to find an easier way. There are times when one has to draw the line on activities and even friendships because they are bad influences. Right decisions will cause a seemingly gloomy, dark, and lonely road when you decide to live your life for Christ which will be a pathway illuminated by the blessing and approval of the Lord. I found that to be true because the closer I draw to the Lord the more, He blessed me. As I stepped out on faith and gave outreach conferences lifting up the name of Jesus Christ. The more He promoted me. Regardless of how dark things may be, we must recognize that there is a resident within us a faith that can guide us through the darkest night. That is what the Lord did when he guided me from the South to the East Coast. From shadows of night to sunlit of light, He, my dear Lord, lifted me out of darkness.

Through all of my mistakes and my heart aches, I went through sorrow and pain, but the Lord Jesus was there, so near and so real. I learned to be contingent on Him so much and grew so much in that experience. Heartache and pain indeed it was. Being a failure at three marriages. Losing my father I had never known such deep sorrow. The Lord was so real to me in my life when I lose my father. I was in Atlanta Georgia in my first marriage when my father died, and my heart dropped when my brother called me because I felt like I never got to tell my dad I was sorry for the way I treated him and I wanted to ask him if he had accepted Jesus Christ in his life. I thought we had time that he would come home and he would be a different person, and I could get to know him, but God said no.

When I got this ray of sunshine in my life after moving to the east coast, I decided if I could touch just one person who was not a Christian. Because my dad was not a Christian, he lived for the world. And I wanted to be a witness to as many as I could reach, trying to lead them to Jesus Christ. Through my outreach ministry. Some family member felt that why are you traveling to different states; it takes money to do that, and you're getting nothing in return. But in my heart, I thought that the Lord was so mighty and gracious to me and I could never repay Him for his saving me. So I'm saying, "Oh my friend, I want you to listen to me, and I want you to hear me clearly get it down plain and straight that the playwright of all suffering and sorrow and pain and death is Satan, not God. God is almighty. God is loving.

And the pain we have in this world is because we live in a world that has been cursed with sin, and if you think that I'm going to line up against God in favor of the devil, and line up with the one who has ultimately wounded me, my family member was so wrong." You know if you would just see that God is evident in nature. God shows Himself as the Father of Lights, and when you look at the sun shining in the sky today, there are some lessons I want you to learn about our great God.

The Word of God according to John has also said in first John chapter one and verse five "God is light, and in Him is no darkness at all." The dark and unhappy times in our life is because we fail to follow the light. The choices I made to marry the men that were in my life was not Gods plan for my life, and it brought me many sleepless nights. Once, I had my freedom again, I choose to give Jesus Christ the light the opportunity to guide me. For eighteen years it has been Jesus, and I walking this journey called life. When you are shielded by the light of Jesus Christ, it is hard for darkness to overtake you.

In my past, I let vulnerability kept me going into one bad relationship after another horrible one. I allowed life decisions defile me, but Jesus is a light that iniquities can't conceal. Reflecting on how Jesus is the light that is that ray of sunshine that has been with me in spite of my downfalls.

Therefore, it's a symbol of Jesus Christ. This light is pure light but wait a minute. This light is powerful, and deliver. Have you ever thought of the power of light? That power saved me from my fallen-self, Jesus Christ delivered me. Oh, my dear friend in John chapter one and verse five, the Bible spoke of the Lord Jesus Christ as being light. And then the Bible says, "And the Light shined in the darkness, and the darkness comprehended it not (did not overtake it).

You can never go into a room with light and turn on darkness. There's no switch where you can turn on the dark. You can always go into a dark room and turn on the light. You see, darkness still has to flee in the presence of light. Light is absolute, totally omnipotent against darkness. By the way, I started my outreach ministry because I wanted to remove darkness out of one person life at a time by spreading the Word about Jesus Christ (the light) across the country. If you're going to get darkness out of a room physically, how are you going to get the darkness out? Are you going to shovel it out? No! Just turn on the light. And the darkness cannot stay. You see there is such power in the name of Jesus Christ the light. And the great God who runs this universe my dear friend knew you in your mother womb. And the sun that shines on us today, tells me of the love of God, and God is concerned about the smallest matters in my life and your life. Oh, the power of light. Darkness cannot stand against it. What incredible force in our awesome God.

Now here's what I want you to think about. Not only the purity of light - it can't be defiled. And it speaks my dear friend of the holiness of our God. The power of light speaks of the omnipotence of God. And then, my dear friend, James says, this light has no variableness. It has no shadow of turning. Now what it means is that this sun never stops shining.

The Bible says that with God, there is no variableness, nor shadow of turning. What He means is God's love never stops shining. But with God, this Sun is always at its brightest, it is always shining down on us. Now, look at it. Every good gift, every perfect gift comes down from above, from the Father of Lights, in whom is no variableness. Now, that means there is no change. That Jesus is the same yesterday, today and forever more. His power will never change. His light will never stop shining in this world.

As you can see I'm excited about the ray of sunshine that Christ has brought into my life, and I can't help but share about His light with you. And so you see that the Bible says that God dwells in light that no man can approach Jesus. But one day we're going to approach unto it because Jesus is the Light of the World and we're going to be made exactly like Him. And when we're shaped exactly like Him, we're in eternity, there is no more time. Time stands still. We're just like Him. But in hell, those in outer darkness, for them time never ends. For us, time stands still. We are like our Lord, we come into the presence of Almighty God, and we are made like Him. Darkness can never stand before light. Light is persistent, it never changes. Never changes in the spiritual realm, as well as in the physical realm. Thank God, for our God who says I change not.

As I close this chapter, please remember every good gift and every perfect gift is from above and cometh down from the father of lights in whom there is no variableness, neither shadow of turning. There is nothing good but what comes from God and only good comes from God. The Father of Lights is God Almighty that shines in our life. As Jesus let His light shine on me, I want to let the brightness from Jesus The light that is on my life shine on you.

When I chose to let, Jesus Christ guide me these eighteen years he has been a ray of sunshine in my life...

I ask you to give him a chance in your life.....

Time for
Change

REMEMBER

WHAT I SAID ABOUT LIGHT?
LIGHT IS PURE,
IT'S IMPOSSIBLE TO DEFILE
LIGHT IS POWERFUL, DARKNESS
CAN NEVER STAND BEFORE IT.
LIGHT IS PERSISTENT, THE LIGHT
NEVER CHANGES.
JESUS CHRIST IS LIGHT

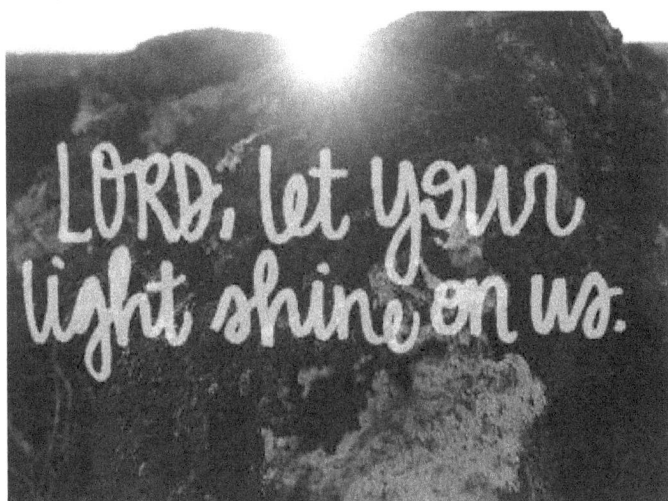

LORD, let your light shine on us.

# *Life Changes*

My life changed after Hurricane Katrina in New Orleans, Louisiana this was a very devastating and life-changing event for my whole family.  My mother, daughter, brother, sister and all of my nieces, nephews, cousins, and aunts. Where still living in New Orleans when this hurricane affected the city.  At that time my baby brother Prophet Michael Allen Ayers Sr. and I had planned an outreach conference in New Orleans in August of 2005. We had guests from Dover, Delaware and we had to ensure that our guests were aboard their plane and on their way home.

Before we could focus on my mom, who was still living there at the time.  My mom did not want to leave her home, but we had to convince my mom to come with us. We left New Orleans on that Sunday, and the hurricane landed in the city on that Tuesday. All of my family's homes were destroyed. After Katrina family members were relocated in other parts of Louisiana, Georgia, Maryland, and Delaware all of their lives had changed.

But most of all my life had changed because after Katrina my mother came and lived with me in Maryland I became a caregiver. I had little and no knowledge of how to be a caregiver. So, I researched the details of being a caregiver what I found is a family member or someone who provides care for a person who needs extra help. My mom fell into that category. All that my mom owned was destroyed by the hurricane.

I had been living in the Metro DC area for five years before this happens. That was a good thing because I was acclimated to my surrounding at that time. I had to make sure my mom had a healthcare professional to ensure her medical care was provided by finding a doctor for her treatment.  Make sure she had all of the medication that the doctor requested and a drugstore that would take my mother's insurance. In general, as a caregiver, I had to focus on my mom daily life activities, which includes grooming, dressing, eating and physical mobility (walking). Once I got all of these things in place after having some time to reflect I realized that my life really had changed.  I was not alone anymore; I had another person that I had to care for besides myself.

 Mistakenly, I assume that there were no resources available to help with these personal tasks and, as a result, I found myself struggling to keep up with errands that I could not handle regularly. I did not have family members and friends to step in to give me this kind of support. I'm going it alone with everyday errands that became increasingly difficult over time. I'm still working a nine to five position, and I have to focus on the demands of my job and always make sure that all of my mom needs are provided as well. I found that the kind of support I was giving was not enough to cover all the necessary bases. Because I traveled for my outreach ministry and my mom is eighty-eight now and going around the country would not be easy for her. I had so many concerns regarding the care of my mom I expressed it with my kids and my brothers, and they told me to have a senior caregiver come in and care for my mom when I had to travel. That helped me in that area, but it did not help me with the neglect of my own enjoyment and health needs. I'm not able to have the freedom as a single person with grown kids who is ready to go out and explore all that life have to offer.

All I'm saying my mom is my queen and I'm truly grateful and bless to have my mother here with me. But just having someone to relieve the burden of driving to appointments to housekeeping and even simple companionship. I hope you do not misunderstand. I love spending time with my mom. I enjoy talking with her and the laughter, but I would like to have the opportunity to have adult companionship of my age group and even of the male persuasion.

I did not have a clue on how to be a caregiver. Ideally, the person who is a caregiver should be compassionated, patient and love seniors in my case. I love my mom dearly and so very blessed to be able to take care of her. I commend all caregivers!

When I left my first husband and started my new position as a Dental Assistant at Charity Hospital. I was hired to go to the operating room and work on surgical dental cases. As you will recall, my three girls where very young so I needed my job. As, I worked a few weeks in the operating room on a rotating schedule with two white girls Patty and Barbara, one black lady who was hired with me. I was made aware that Patty and Barbara would go home after they would complete their surgical duties. Will that was not the case for the new lady and myself we had to return to the clinic and work in the dental clinic after our surgical cases. The new employee did not want to say anything because she was new regarding Patty and Barbara going home after surgical cases. I felt differently, I was hired the same time the new employee but I was not going to work surgical cases and not be able to go home like these young ladies. I spoke with my supervisor Willie Mae Jet, who did not take my concerns seriously. I took my concerns to her supervisor who happen to be a white male and he made change regarding my making him aware that if I was not given the same privilege or if these young ladies was not made to return to the clinic like I had to return to work on general dental patience. Than I would take it to a higher authority, as you can imagine I was not a well like employee in the dental clinic. Being new I could have lost my position but that was a chance I was willing to take to be treated fairly.

Other life changes are ones that I made happen like the time my Chrysler was repossessed after I had moved from Louisiana to Silver Spring, MD and accepted my new position in the Washington, DC area as a Paralegal, I with up against the finance company and was able to get them to return my car into my possession. After Katrina, my oldest daughter and her husband moved to Houston, TX and my daughter Toyota was repossessed by the bank in Louisiana I when up against that bank and they returned my daughter her car. I when in the Silver Spring courtroom and represented myself Pro se against Verizon Phone Company and the judge awarded my judgment. My sister had a case against Wal-Mart, and I assisted her, and they settled with my sister. I wanted my sister to obtain a lawyer. Because the evidence that was similar to her case was awarded millions, but my sister did not want to, but I didn't want her not to go after Wal-Mart, so I assisted her.

I recently with after the Hammond, Louisiana police department that put my nephew through police brutality. They let my nephew out of jail alive. They may not have been entirely fair to my nephew, but he walks out of that jail alive. I when up against my superior on my job and God brought me out with a promotion and leadership detail assignment.

Romans 12:2 Do not conform to the pattern of this world, but be transformed by the renewing of your mind. Then you will be able to test and approve what God's will is—his good, pleasing and perfect will.

Life will always bring us through changes as you can see from the changes that I just expounded on above, but the most significant difference is about changing your mind from doubt to believing. If we do not believe and have faith that our situation can change and that Jesus Christ will move on our behalf. I had to have faith for the things that I expressed above to come out favorably. I had to have faith that God would hear my prayers that Jesus Christ would move on my behalf. What I'm saying is belief will change your life. Like myself, I would like to change my arms; they are large, and I do not like the way they appear.

Imagine, you could transform anything about yourself, where would you start? Lots of us would start on the outside. If you could wave a magic wand and change your outward appearance, would it be a light touch-up or an extreme makeover? Would we even recognize you? I think we all go through periods where we desperately want to change our outward appearance. We diet obsessively and work out, which is good for our health but can be a losing battle because after we lose that weight and finally look good, it tends to come creeping back again.

Finally, you reach the juncture in life where it's easier to try to cover it up than to lose it simply. In extreme cases, we may just give up altogether and stop caring about how we look. But as hard as it is to modify on the outside, it seems extremely harder to improve on the inside. If there is anything we know about humans, it is that people change slowly, if they change at all. It is more important to change your mind; you should focus on your belief system. Having faith in yourself is a start, but additionally, you must have faith in God and His son Christ Jesus. Who is able to change any adverse situation in your life as you can see from the changes that he made for me?

I believed I had faith and Jesus Christ turned negative situations to positive changes. Change is very crucial as I wrote in my book entitled Waiting for Change. Especially, when it comes to women, men and children living in an abusive situation as I was at one point in my life.

# ABUNDANT LIFE

*I can't wait to start working at living.*
*Life is so precious, and it fades away so*
*quickly.*
*We should grab hold*
*To every moment that God gives us.*
*Walking in that abundant life that*

*God Promises*

*Family*

*Where life starts*

*And*

*Love begins…*

Time
spent with family
is worth every
Second

# *Fun and Family Time*

Family time is significant to me, and I try to spend as much time as I can with my kids and my grandkids. These are memorable times with my family. All my kids were together for my son graduation from undergrad and graduate school 2018. We all traveled to New York after my son graduated from undergrad 2008 and with on the Ellis Island Ferry ride. Activities I like to have with my kids is to go to new places we never visit before. My son and daughter-in-law brought me to Niagara Falls and Toronto Canada for mother's day May 2018 we all enjoy traveling. The trip to Canada It was so much fun because we were together as a family, and we visit a dinosaur park, my grandson, Christian loved it because dinosaurs are his favorite. That's one of the things we like to do together as a family visit new places and new restaurants.

Another activity my family enjoys is going to the beach. The kids have taken me to Rehoboth Beach in Delaware, Ocean City Beach in Maryland and Virginia Beach in Virginia they enjoy swimming in the water, we appreciate playing in the sand, and spending time together. We have been to the water park in New Jersey to Orlando, Florida Disney World and Six Flag in Maryland. During the summers going to the beach, with my family was so much fun. A pastime or activity my family likes to do together is play board games. Especially, I love to play with my grandkids Mariah and Christian they do not want to lose the game ever.

I love this because when it's my turn, I win when I'm not letting them win. A favorite activity that my family does is have BBQs in the summer. In the backyard, the kids will play slip and slide in the water, it is funny to watch! My grandkids playing with each other in the water. One significant time we had a family reunion in 2017in New Orleans, Louisiana, it was great to have my kids there minus two, but it was so exciting to have my mother family the Gilbert's all together for the first time. My favorite free time with the kids is watching a movie. We curl up with a  bowl of popcorn and get cozy. We fight over a soft throw blanket.

I always fall asleep. Other favorite times with my family is when we spend time together in New Orleans for Mardi Gras because it is always great to go home and eat some delicious food. Going back and having a Po- Boy sandwich and Big Shot drink. My kids have brought me to New Jersey to the Statue of Liberty. When my brother Wilbert came to visit me, it was fun bringing him to New York and Philadelphia to eat at this cozy breakfast spot a memorable time for me.

Family time is priceless the time that you have with your family is the time you can't replace. Having Thanksgiving dinners and Christmas cook-offs is special times that I'm looking forward to having more time like those. My kids gave me a 60th birthday party at home in New Orleans, Louisiana and all of my kids was there, my brothers, minus my sister but all of my nieces and nephews. Many of my family members were there; it was a fantastic time unforgettable.

Some of my kids and grandkids are so far away from me in Tucson, Arizona and Houston, Texas but now that I will be retired, I will be able to spend more time with them. Missing Robert Jr., Ronnie, Rhea, Royal and Chloe and I have enjoyed my time here in Maryland with Marques Jr., Markel, Mariah, and Christian.

Commuting on the train to work every day I became close to some friends that rode the train into Washington, DC with me daily. This was another fun time in my life that I spend with my train bubbies. We had a bond and started a birthday celebration club. We would take each other out for their birthday to these upscale white tablecloth restaurants where we paid up to 1000 dollars for our dinner. We each would take a turn purchasing a birthday cake these where some elaborate cakes such as a Martini glass, a Gucci purse some beautiful, extravagant cakes. I'm going to miss the fantastic time with Candace, Thomas, Darlene, William, Tinuke, and Shawn. These young people made me welcome into their world. I also, will not forget Phoelicia and Dana to young ladies I have adopted as my east coast family.

Some fantastic ladies that came into my life and supported my first book signing Patricia, Beverly, Barbara, Janice, Angela, and Stacey. I do not want to forget Yvonne who God placed her as the guardian angel, and I'm asking God to pay her back double fold. God put Yvonne in a position to overthrow adverse action by my superiors. You meet lovely people as you go through life and these ladies made my east coast stay memorable.

The exciting five years, I have had with Team La'Shaes these savvy businesswomen has been truly phenomenal, and I have been having fun with them making me feel like I'm young as them. My two daughters Lakiesha, CEO and La'Shone, Business Manager the team Jayda, Stacey, Shanericka, Sarah, Toni, Krystal, Alisa, Crystal, and Barbara. Some team members who are no longer with us are Barbara, Camiko, Rohanda, Ms. Tracey, Yolanda, Ashley, Michelle, Shenika and Charmese. Thanking La'Shaes for whom I'm the underwriter and very proud of these business moguls, and for the enjoying time, I have spent with them. Looking for many more years of great success.

I want to mention Minister Michelle Duplessis my first author for my publishing company Reach The Press, and she has joined the Women of Distinction Outreach Ministry, along with two other dynamic Women of God Dr. Trisha Johnson, and Elder Stacey Bulluck. All are anointed trailblazer for the Lord. Evangelist Pamela Smith who has fellowship with WOD. A young lady I met visiting my daughter in Houston, TX and the Lord gave me a word for this young lady. I had never seen her before or ever met her before, I wasn't going to give her the message from the Lord because I said she just came over to have a conversation with my daughter, but the anointing was so intense. What God gave her is her testimony and for her to tell but I'm so proud that she is kicking the door down on the devil she is a powerhouse for the Lord. Two other great Women of God is Prophetess Valencia Boyd Luckett and First Lady Sheilah Olds that have been a great support to my ministry. So, very thankful for my Pastor Edd Olds and Pastor Devin and First Lady Mya Stephenson for their support of my Women of Distinction Outreach Ministries.

My brother Prophet Michael Allen Ayers Sr. Is a family member who has been very instrumental in my life and my ministry? He was the one who helped me move to the Washington, DC area. We have been traveling and conducting ministry outreach across this country from young. I'm so grateful for my brother because he never compromises with me so for all of you who Prophet Ayers has come with and in your face message, I was no exception. When I was downtrodden and having doubt Mike would call me and ask where your faith is, stop having a pity party and do what God has for you to do. Mike is a praying man that is always lifting our family up in prayer. But I miss my sister Wanda her and me when we were young was the dynamic duo that was praying for our whole family. My dad to stop drinking, my mom for God to keep her safe, my brothers to bring them out of the world. Because my dad had influenced them so much when my dad would have them driving him around to bars for him to drink. My sister was so anointed that she could see demons and could call them by names, and I know that some of you reading my book is going to say.

What! See Demons. Yes! For you all that do not believe that the devil has a legion, as well as God, have a Host of Angels then you're mistaken. My sister places her hand on my brother Wilbert's head at one of our Sunday Service at Temple of Prayer with Prophet Samuel, and my brother was touch by the Holy Spirit. Wanda, a Powerhouse let the cares of this world overtake her but don't you know that I'm asking God. Do it again touch her life again bringing this dynamic Woman of God on the scene, so when she put her feet on the floor, the devil will know that she has a panoramic view of his demonic forces and going to destroy his plot and plans.

My oldest brother Wilbert put his mantle down, but I'm asking God again for His anointed power to touch and bring this Man of God back to his first love preaching God Word. As you can see my mother, my two grandmothers were praying for my sibling, and I, the devil think that he has knocked down part of this camp, but long as I have breath, I'm praying for my sister and brother to come back into the assembly of Jesus Christ. If you're a prayer warrior, I ask you to pray with me for this Woman of God my sister Wanda Ayers and my brother Prophet Wilbert Ayers Jr.

As I close this chapter take time out to be with family because we are not promised tomorrow. I praying for a long life so that I can have many more family fun days with my family, kids, grandkids, and friends. Remember time is not standing still so enjoy every minute, second and every hour with your family.

Fun in the Sun is waiting for me……..

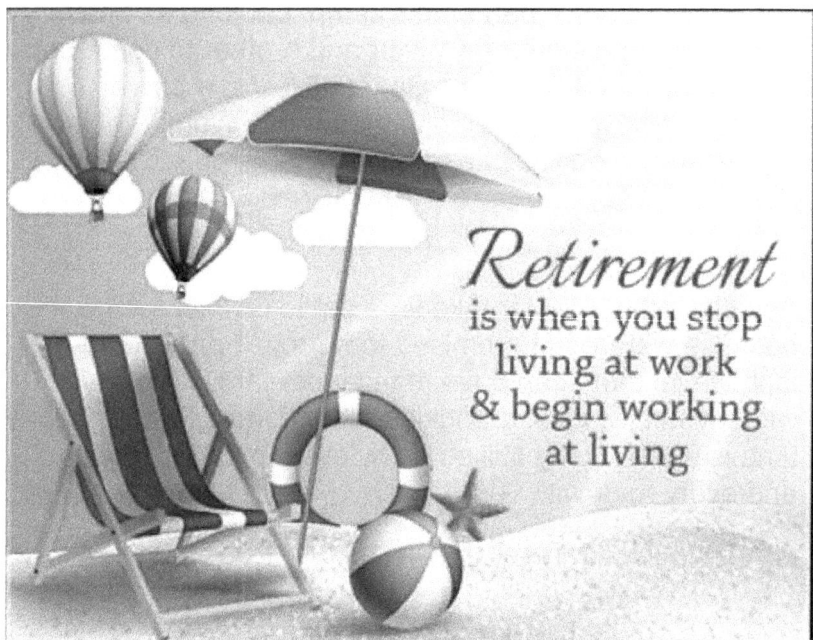

Retirement
is when you stop
living at work
& begin working
at living

# *Retirement*

Just hearing the word retirement is a mesmerizing image of leisurely activities. While such pursuits bring a certain amount of gratification, I want to spend my latter years in exceptional service to a cause greater than my personal pleasure. I want to know how God wants me to use my talents and life experiences. My decisions about retirement I want to make a routine that includes my ministry before I become too comfortable in leisurely activities.  As a baby boomer approaching retirement, as an educated, capable, and eager adult I want to seek ways to use my skills in the church. I'm willing to volunteer, ready to rise to a task if challenged. I hope that my outreach ministry as a retiree will meet essential needs.  It is my goal to service others versus living for myself. Jesus said for us to be our brother's keeper is the motive for my selfless act of using my time, talent, and skill for the benefit of others. I have worked for over forty years now I come to the end of my working career as I walk through the door of retirement.

I want to step in the shoes of a minister full time. A minister is quite simply, one who acts on behalf of others. In much the same way my ministry belongs to Jesus Christ, and I represent Him as His minister.

Ministry isn't a possession that belongs to us, but a call we obey, a service we carry out for others. Ministry always fosters on the work of others that is why I started the Alabaster Box Fellowship so that I can encourage and build up other young men and women in ministry. My ministry Women of Distinction Outreach is a ministry without walls. You see many people join the minister rather than the church or ministry.

People join a ministry because the minister is a spellbinding preacher or a compassionate pastor or an attractive personality. The problem is that when the minister in time shows the inevitable flaws, they become disenchanted their ties to the church or ministry are flimsy because they have joined the leader and not the ministry. I hope that my outreach ministry will be the embodiment of the Gospel and my followers will not be following me the leader but Jesus Christ.

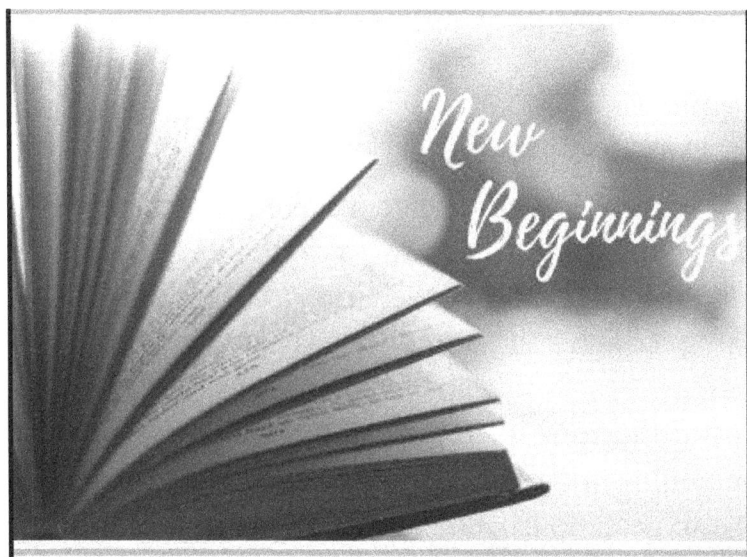

New Beginnings

# New Beginning

We all mess up. We say things we later wish we could take back. We do things we wish we could undo. We miss opportunities. This happens in all parts of our lives. Sometimes we make mistakes, occasionally we hurt the people we love, and sometimes we dishearten God. And since we all mess up, we like to start over—to turn our backs on the past, to look forward, to hope that this time around, things are going to be better. Something is exciting about starting over—new challenges, new experiences, and new opportunities. I'm looking ahead to a new beginning in my retirement. I have plans, things I'd like to accomplish, challenges ahead of me. Looking back over the past, I realize there are some affairs I'd want to do differently. Perhaps you've had similar thoughts... I remember what it was like for me to start a new position the anticipation of meeting new people and starting new projects. I'm not so different than others. I think individuals generally like to start over. I suspect that's why some people are continuously starting new relationships. These new relationships maybe business, friendship and family relationships that they start over. Conceivably that's why we all like opportunities to rededicate our lives to God.

Yes, we all like to begin over. Why? Because what's in store holds the expectation for a lot better. But things don't always stay this way. After too many disappointments we often give up, we lose confidence. A person can only start over so many times before you begin to wonder, "What's the point? What makes you think you're not going to mess it up again?" For some, there is no starting over. No new start. No new beginning. They have accepted their life as a failure. They have learned to live without hope. It's tragic to admit, but many have reached this place of hopelessness. After too many disappointments, it can happen to anyone. After a while, you may begin to feel that there just isn't a new beginning for you.

However, the Bible does not agree with this belief. In stark contrast the Bible speaks of an entirely new beginning: **(2 Cor. 5:17)** Therefore, if anyone is in Christ, he is a new creation; the old has gone, the new has come!

That means that when someone has decided to dedicate their lives to Jesus, Jesus begins a new act of creation in their lives. They aren't merely reformed or rehabilitated. No, they are recreated. They become a brand-new person from within, and they begin a brand-new life.

For Christ's love compels us, because we are convinced that Jesus died for all, and therefore all disappointments and failures are conquered. And he died for all, that those who live should no longer live for themselves but for him who died for them and was raised again. **(2 Cor. 5:14-15).** When I was eight years old and was baptized by Pastor Freddie H. Dunn, General Overseer of New Hope Baptist Church, in New Orleans, Louisiana. This is what baptism symbolizes. Your old life dies, and you are buried under the water, just as Jesus was buried in the tomb. Then you stand up out of the water, just as Jesus stood up from the grave. You stand up as a new person, a new beginning. That's why Paul can confidently say "the old has gone, the new has come!"

When we refer to our Bible, we see that Jesus offered just this sort of new life to the hopeless. Throughout the Word, Jesus offers us living water—the living water which quenches a person's thirst and gives eternal life.

There're some Old Testament texts which refer to God as the fountain of living water (Ps 36:9; Jer. 17:13), and in making this reference to living water, Jesus is actually telling us, "Hey, I'm the Messiah! I'm what you've been longing for! I'm what you need in your life!"

It's not easy to confront our failures, our disappointments, and our hurt. In fact, it's possible for us to get used to living in spiritual and physical poverty, to live without hope. To hope again is scary. If we begin to expect again, we can be disappointed again. If we try to start over once more, we might just fail once more. That is my fear about going into retirement. I made so many mistakes I don't want to repeat. But however frightening it might be to think of building a new start that is precisely what the Bible is promising. I'm going to stand on the promises of God and believe that my new beginning is going to be great.

When we make that decision to give ourselves wholeheartedly to Christ, and He begins that work of recreation in us, we become His ambassadors!

As I walk through that door of retirement, I want to be an ambassador for Christ. Where Jesus Christ can entrust in me the message of reconciliation spreading His gospel across this nation. Suddenly my life has a larger purpose than just relaxing and living comfortably. When we meet Jesus as our personal Savior, then our lives are filled with a deeper meaning, then we become His ambassadors, then we are entrusted with the message of reconciliation. Perhaps things are going well.

Sure, I've made some mistakes, I've messed up a little, but I'm still living with the optimism that I will be able to start over, my retirement presents me with the perfect opportunity to turn over a new leaf—to drop some bad eating habits and pick up some good ones. I'm confident that there will be new opportunities and a new beginning awaits me. It doesn't really matter where you are today, because today is a new day. Tomorrow is the new possibilities.

# Close Door

As I open the door to retirement, I want to close the door to my career.  I do not want to forget my time spend in the United States Air Force for four years as an Inventory Management Specialist it was lovely to travel the US to San Antonio, Texas,  Denver Colorado and near San Francisco, California. The times, I spend in the Air Force gave me the opportunity to go to Oakland, California, Los Angeles, California, Sacramento, California and Vallejo, California. To give you a glimpse of my working career. That I'm so happy to leave behind.  As a teen, I worked at Schwegmann Supermarket as a cashier in New Orleans. I worked at the Center for Disease Control in Atlanta, Georgia for a short time.  I attended Dental Assisting School and Paralegal College in New Orleans, Louisiana. I worked for Charity Hospital, New Orleans for nine years in the dental clinic as a Dental Assistant and a Dental Scrub nurse in the operating room. I worked for the Department of Veterans Affairs, Medical Center, New Orleans, Louisiana as a Dental Assistant, Procurement Technician, and a Lead Inventory Management Specialist for fourteen years.  I worked one year at the State Attorney General Office, New Orleans, Louisiana as a Paralegal.

I have been here in Metro Washington, DC area for eighteen years working for the Department of Veteran Affairs, Headquarters as a Paralegal, Deputy Director Human Resources and Portfolio Manager all of this helped me provide for my kids and myself but was never my first love.

My first love was going out and preaching God's Word. Now, I will be able to commit to my first love and enjoy want I do and not dread it like I did when I had to go to work every day. The truth is, God wants us to enjoy life every day. God approves of us enjoying our lives, take a look at John 10:10. It says the thief comes only to steal and kill and destroy. Jesus came that we may have and enjoy life, and have it in abundance (to the full, till it overflows). God the Father and Jesus Christ, the son, doesn't just want us to be alive, but He wants us to enjoy being active. Jesus wants us to live with joy – abundant, overflowing joy.

That is what I'm looking forward to that abundant life. My passion as a preacher of God's Word is to help people learn how to live the life Jesus died to give us. And I've learned through my own life experience that if you don't have joy, then no matter what you have or what you do or how great your circumstances may be...it doesn't mean much.

So how do we get the joy of the Lord? Jesus tells us in John fifteen that if we abide in Him, we will experience God's will for our lives, and everything Jesus has will be ours. Abiding means making Jesus the most eminent person in my life, living and remaining in Him, and making everything in life revolve around Jesus Christ. That's when we bear the fruit of a godly life. And that's when God's real joy is made available in us. It's easy to see that focusing on Jesus has so many benefits. For one, when we're paying attention to Him, we won't be focused on the problems in the world; and we'll be able to live with God's peace and joy. Another benefit of living this way is that it keeps us from being continually stressed-out, living in survival mode and just getting through the day. My entire career, I was living in survival mode just getting through the day.

Don't Wait on "When..."So many individuals have the mindset that they will be delighted and enjoy life when...when they go on vacation when the kids are a grownup when they get a promotion at work when they get married...the list could go on and on. I can relate to this because there was a time when even though I was successful in my job, I wasn't enjoying the daily responsibilities and activities it involved.

I had to learn to live in the moment and enjoy what God was doing in me and through me now, not when my outreach conference was over or when I could go on vacation. God wants me to enjoy my life now, not when. I'm so thankful that we have the Holy Spirit, who lives in every believer in Jesus Christ. He is the Helper who gives us strength and anointing to live this ordinary, day-to-day life with the joy of the Lord.

Nehemiah 8:10 says the joy of the Lord is our strength.

And we need that strength every day.  It's important to understand what happiness is living life every day. It's not about entertaining yourself all the time, getting your way all the time or laughing all the time. Joy can be the extreme cheerful or calm delight and everything in between! The Bible says in Proverbs 17:22 that "a happy heart is good medicine and a cheerful mind works healing...." Laughter relieves pain and creates a sense of well-being. It can raise your energy level, relieve tension and replace your attitude. No wonder the devil wants to steal our joy and get us discouraged, depressed and downtrodden.

Remember that the thief comes only to steal, kill and destroy. But we don't have to give in to him and lose our joy. In my career, I had times, where I felt discouraged because of the mistreatment by superiors that put a damper on my life, but Jesus was my joy. He brought me through those hindrances.

 I look forward to closing this chapter in my working career. Remembering, God wants us to enjoy life every day.

*Turning the pages in Life*

*Is*

*The scenery of*

*a*

# NEW VIEW

# Retirement

# DEDICATION

I dedicate this book to my kids I hope that they will forgive me for the many mistakes that I made. All of the unpleasant things that I may have put them through. I'm so happy that they did not follow in my footsteps and obeying the Word of God regarding marriage. Understanding that love and forgiveness is the key to a lasting relationship.

To my grandkids do not be a follower be a leader. Be the ones that create the trends, fashion the fad and let everyone follow them. I want them all to know that I love them very much. I know I do not say it enough, but I Love them with all my heart.......

*Love your Mom*

**Jesus Christ is my guide on this journey...**

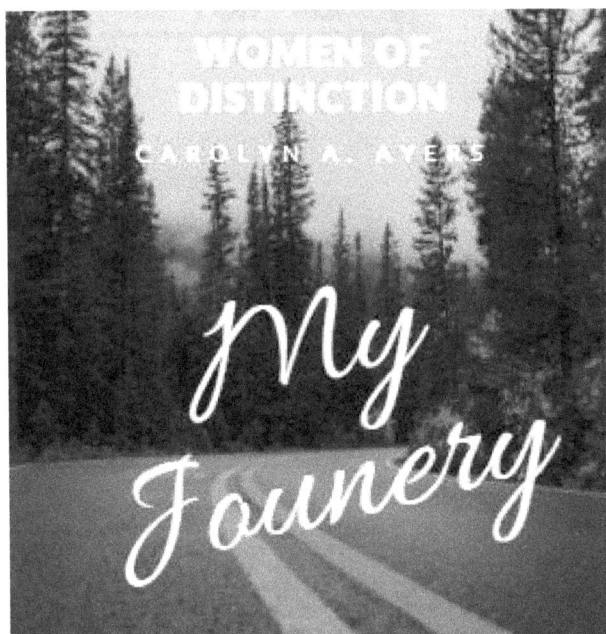

WOMEN OF
DISTINCTION

CAROLYN A. AYERS

My
Jouney

www.ingramcontent.com/pod-product-compliance
Lightning Source LLC
Chambersburg PA
CBHW060651150426
42813CB00052B/587